WORK FOR YOURSELF

BULLET GUIDE

Matt Avery

Hodder Education, 338 Euston Road, London NW1 3BH

Hodder Education is an Hachette UK company

First published in UK 2011 by Hodder Education

This edition published 2011

Copyright © 2011 Matt Avery

The moral rights of the author have been asserted

Database right Hodder Education (makers)

Artworks (internal and cover): Peter Lubach

Cover concept design: Two Associates

British Library Cataloguing in Publication Data: a catalogue record for this title is available from the British Library.

10 9 8 7 6 5 4 3 2 1

The publisher has used its best endeavours to ensure that any website addresses referred to in this book are correct and active at the time of going to press. However, the publisher and the author have no responsibility for the websites and can make no guarantee that a site will remain live or that the content will remain relevant, decent or appropriate.

The publisher has made every effort to mark as such all words which it believes to be trademarks. The publisher should also like to make it clear that the presence of a word in the book, whether marked or unmarked, in no way affects its legal status as a trademark.

Every reasonable effort has been made by the publisher to trace the copyright holders of material in this book. Any errors or omissions should be notified in writing to the publisher, who will endeavour to rectify the situation for any reprints and future editions.

Hachette UK's policy is to use papers that are natural, renewable and recyclable products and made from wood grown in sustainable forests. The logging and manufacturing processes are expected to conform to the environmental regulations of the country of origin.

www.hoddereducation.co.uk

Typeset by Stephen Rowling/Springworks

Printed in Spain

To the best company secretary in the business

Acknowledgements

My sincere thanks to everyone who contributed to this book with case studies, top tips and invaluable insight; and to those whose encouragement and support made it possible, especially Alison and Victoria at Hodder Education, and Suze.

About the author

Matt Avery began working for himself in 1997 when he established his first business, a marketing consultancy. Having been 'bitten by the bug' of being answerable only to himself (not to mention keeping all the rewards of his hard work!), a second company followed in 2001, this time a copywriting agency.

Today, Matt consults on a number of companies in a wide variety of industries, as well as writing business books on the subject of going it alone in the workplace and setting up and running successful businesses. Matt also gives lectures and workshops as well as motivational talks.

Contents

Introduction

'If you think you can or think you can't, you're right.'
Henry Ford

Self-belief is one of the most important factors when **working for yourself**. Another is having at your disposal all the **insider know-how, shortcuts, top tips** and **best practice knowledge** to give **you** and **your business** the very best possible chance of **success**.

Working for yourself **isn't easy** – 95 per cent of all small businesses **fail** within the first five years – but **you can stack the odds in your favour** if you know how. Key to this are:

* understanding the realities and requirements of working for yourself
* robust, realistic planning and preparation.

vi

By getting the **inside track** to working for yourself you'll be giving **yourself** and **your business** every chance of **success**. You'll need plenty of **determination** to see it through, but if you do you'll soon discover that **being your own boss** is the most **rewarding** career of all.

The **opportunity to *decide*** what you do, when, how and where you do it, to **dictate your future**, and to **keep all the rewards** of your hard work is one that few of us can resist – as **more than 3 million** people in the UK alone have already discovered!

If you're ready to **quit the rat race** and **take control of your career,** this book will guide you through all the necessary steps and provide you with all the **ammunition** you need to successfully begin **working for yourself**.

1 Do you have what it takes to work for yourself?

Going solo: should you take the plunge?

You may dream of working for yourself, but do you have what it takes to go solo? Will you thrive, or will you soon tire of the novelty? Do you have the **personality**, **approach** and **outlook** to succeed?

The move to becoming your own boss can certainly be **exhilarating** and **liberating**, but it can also be **daunting** and even **terrifying**.

Do you have what it takes to go solo?

This chapter will help you explore the issues you should consider before you take the plunge, and covers the following questions:

* Do you have the **right personality** to be your own boss?
* Who do you think you are and who do you want to be?
* Do you understand your key personality traits?
* What is **psychometric profiling** and is it really for you?
* Who uses psychometric profiling?
* Is there a 'right' personality type for working solo?
* Which **path** should you choose?

Once you have the answers to these questions, you will be able to decide whether it's a good idea for you to take the next step towards working for yourself.

Do you have the right personality to be your own boss?

You may have long dreamed of working for yourself, but in order to decide whether you have **what it takes** to go solo, you first need to ask yourself:

> **'Some people dream of success...while others wake up and work hard at it.'**
> Anon.

Am I the sort of person who will thrive working on my own every day?

Am I prepared to fight to secure work?

Will I soon tire of the novelty of being my own boss?

Am I confident I can manage my own time and abilities to ensure that my company succeeds?

Do I have the personality, approach and outlook to thrive while working on my own?

Who do you think you are?

The change to solo working affects not only your work life but **your life in general**, and it's important that the **potential benefits** to be gained outweigh the **risks** involved in your particular case. Respondents to a recent study said working for themselves had made them:

* happier
* healthier
* nicer to know
* friendlier

Top tip
The real question is not '**Where** do you want to be in the future?' nor even '**What** do you want to be?' It's '**Who** do you want to be?'

* more relaxed
* liberated
* more in control
* wiser.

Who do you want to be?
And do you have what it takes?

Understanding your personality traits

Understanding your key **personality traits** will
help you to see your work life **strengths** and
weaknesses, and any areas that may **need
development**.

* What assets/hindrances will you
  bring to your new career?
* What support might you need?
* What changes will you need to
  make to your current lifestyle?
* What additions to your skill set
  may be required?
* What personality traits might you
  need to work on?

What is psychometric profiling?

The best way to understand **your personality** and how it corresponds to the **workplace** is to take a **psychometric profiling test**, many of which can now be found online. These tests will:

* apply psychological measurement to determine your **primary personality traits**
* measure your **attitudes** and **aptitudes**
* help you determine whether you have the right **personality type** and the necessary **drive** to work for yourself
* qualify and quantify your work life **skills**
* help identify the areas in which you are **weak** or to which you are not suited.

Remember
* Answer the questions honestly and accurately.
* The results are for your eyes only.
* There are no 'right' or 'wrong' answers.

Is psychometric profiling really for me?

If you love the **idea** of working for yourself but you're not sure whether you would **love** it or **hate** it in **reality**, then a **psychometric profiling study** might help you to determine your **best course of action**.

An accurate psychometric profile will help you understand:

1 more about yourself
2 whether you are likely to find the transition to becoming your own boss easy or difficult
3 the areas you may need to work on if you are to become a successful soloist.

Forewarned is forearmed
The more you know about yourself, the better you can prepare yourself and your business for the journey ahead.

Who uses psychometric profiling?

If you have never heard of psychometric profiling or are not sure how useful it really is, you might be interested to know that **psychometric profile tests**:

* form a **fundamental** part of recruitment for **many large companies**
* are used by **more than 95 per cent** of companies in the **FTSE 100**
* afford employers an **insight** into the personality types of prospective and current employees
* are used to **evaluate** their employees' **ongoing happiness** in their jobs.

Many people who successfully leave paid employment to work for themselves do so initially as the result of psychometric profiling tests administered by their employer, with results suggesting they would be happier working for themselves!

The 'right' personality type for solo working

Remember that there is no one **'right'** or even preferable **personality type** – it is the presence or absence of key traits that is important. **Psychometric profiling** will help you identify such things as:

your **approach** to your home and work life

your **communication** style

your **attitude** to work

your ability to **get on** with others

your **motivation**, **determination** and **perseverance**

your **social** skills

your preferred **working styles**

your **assertiveness**

your **willingness** to take instruction and your **ability** to follow it

your attitude towards **authority**

how quick you are to make **assumptions**

your **self-reliance**

your ability to demonstrate **flexibility** in your working life.

Choosing your path

'He who is outside his door has the hardest part of his journey behind him.'

Dutch proverb

You have decided to **forge a new career** path – so what will it be? The **same** work as you are used to or a completely **new career**? There are four basic choices:

a same work, different company
b different work, same company
c different work, different company
d same/different work but working for yourself.

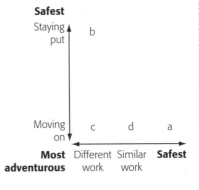

You need to balance safety and security with adventure.

2 What working for yourself actually means

What's involved

Working for yourself means **taking charge** of your working life and creating, often from scratch, the **structure** you think you'll need in your day-to-day working life – and then rigorously **testing** it. Carefully think through everything you will need to create a defined **workplace structure** that works for you. Remember, you're the boss – so the buck stops with you.

You're the boss – so the buck stops with you

What's **involved** in working for yourself?
This chapter looks at:

* what to think about when
  setting up your business
* the **benefits** – and **traps** – of
  being your **own boss**
* envisaging the **route** to take
* planning and preparation
  (the six Ps)
* creating the **right impression**
  with a logo and stationery
* what you need to know in order
  to turn your **passion** into your **job**
* **fine tuning** your offer.

The requirements of working for yourself

'The way to get started is to quit talking and begin doing.'
Walt Disney

You will need to carefully **think through** all the steps you must take for your business to **hit the ground running** from the outset, such as:

16

* your preferred working structure
* knowing what work you will be doing for whom, and when
* how you will attract clients
* putting a support system in place for advice and assistance
* providing cover if you fall ill.

Top tip
The quantity of effort you put in now will be directly reflected in the quality of your business when it launches.

The benefits – and traps – of working for yourself

Working for yourself means you can:

✔ work your own **hours**
✔ take **holidays** when you please
✔ **pick and choose** your clients
✔ keep all the **rewards** of your efforts.

But it also means you can't:

✘ rely on **admin** support
✘ **sit back** and wait for the work to roll in
✘ expect others to do the **jobs you hate**
✘ **afford** to get things wrong, e.g. insurances, tax and VAT returns, bank accounts, IT.

'Failing to plan means planning to fail. What are your goals?'
Anon.

Envisaging the route

Envisaging only the **big picture** is not enough. Knowing how you want your company to **look, feel** and be **defined** is good, but you must be clear about **how** you'll achieve this, and how the company will **operate from day to day**.

Top tip
Planning ahead in the early stages can save you headaches and wasted time further down the track.

CASE STUDY: Planning ahead

'You must be prepared and think it through from every angle, the requirements and practicalities of your new working life, all the boring bits! I had thought it through very carefully, looking at each stage in turn but there were still some surprises.' (Self-employed consultant, USA)

The six Ps

'The six Ps: Proper Planning and Preparation Prevent Poor Performance.'

Charlie Batch

Why do you want to start your own business?

How determined are you to succeed?

How much hard work are you willing to put in?

Every year **thousands of businesses fail** due to the lack of:

* a clear **vision**
* a long-term **strategy**
* a detailed **business plan**
* establishing the business's **day-to-day goals** and needs.

Give yourself plenty of time to get things organized and you will be giving yourself and your business every chance of succeeding.

Creating the right impression

It is worth investing in a good **logo** to give your new company a **head start**. A good logo will:

> A picture speaks a thousand words.

* make your company's name stand out
* make it visually memorable
* be a reflection of your company's brands and values
* give prospective clients a feel for what sort of company it is.

It can also **communicate** your company's offer. For example:

1 Is it a service?
2 Are you a supplier?
3 Are you a consultant?

You can then use your logo to **stamp your company's identity** on all your stationery.

Baby steps

Once you have your **logo**, you will need to order your **stationery**, but first:

1 decide your **budget**
2 list your **target** for client capture and/or sales
3 ensure that both are **realistic**.

Top tip
Allotting too much of your initial budget to advertising and marketing puts unnecessary pressure on your business's finances, risking cash-flow problems.

Common reasons for overspend are:

* over-excitement about your new business
* eagerness to announce your company's arrival
* desire to get known quickly
* fear of not generating income quickly enough
* desire to impress your friends and family.

Initially, you should only invest in **sufficient** promotional materials to **raise awareness** of your company.

Turning your passion into your job

Is making a **career** from your **hobby** realistic or just a pipe dream? Having done your research, answer the following questions honestly.

1   Is there definitely a **need** for your offer?
2   Is there **room** in the **marketplace**?
3   Are you providing/creating anything **unique**?
4   How **frequently** is your offer likely to be taken up?
5   How much will you be able to **charge**, and will this give you a **profit**?
6   Is your offer **sustainable** for the long term?

If the answers to all these questions are positive, and you already have some actual and potential clients, then **workplace nirvana** might just be a realistic possibility.

Is making a career from your hobby realistic?

22

Fine tuning your offer

Warning!
To make your new career workable, you may have to accept compromises along the way. Don't assume that people will readily pay you to pursue your passion precisely the way you want. If you can't pursue your hobby exactly as you would wish, is it still preferable to other work?

Hobby

Will only ever be...

Fun only required

Means need to make money elsewhere ← Doesn't produce much money

Hobby

Is new full-time...

Fun diminished

Only required source of revenue ← Generates income

3 Setting up your solo work life

The importance of the workplace environment

The positive impact of working in an inspiring environment is difficult to overstate. You will feel **energized** and **excited** every time you arrive at your workplace.

Equally, settling for somewhere mediocre is a sure way to curb your enthusiasm and handicap your business's potential. If you cannot find anything exactly right, make some improvements to your working environment yourself.

The positive impact of working in an inspiring environment is difficult to overstate

This chapter looks at the issues around choosing your **work environment**. Deciding where to work depends on several factors, not least of which is finding the right situation for your particular type of business. The options, which all have **benefits** and potential **drawbacks**, are:

* **working from home**
* **sharing** an office
* **renting** an office – possibly a good short-term solution
* **buying** an office – as an investment for the long term.

Where to work?

The exact **requirements** of your working **environment** will depend on the **type of work** you intend to pursue:

Is it specialized?

What looks and feels right for your business?

Can you work from home?

Are your first premises likely to be short or long term?

Is it preferable to work alongside other like-minded people or to have your own space?

> **Top tip**
> Finding the right premises is crucial to the success of your business.

Working from home

To most people this seems like the **obvious** and the **best** choice. However, there are both **advantages** and **disadvantages** to working from home.

Advantages

- ✔ *Everything you require will be to hand*
- ✔ *No more **commuting***
- ✔ *Erstwhile commuting **time** can be spent working*
- ✔ *The **comforts** of home to enjoy all day*
- ✔ *Cost **savings***

Disadvantages

- ✘ *Multiple **distractions***
- ✘ *The **battle** to keep your home/work lives **separate***
- ✘ ***Losing** the mental **transition time** commuting provides*
- ✘ ***Increased pressure** on self-motivation and self-discipline*
- ✘ *Isolation*

It's important to **explore all the options** open to you. Is working from home really the best solution?

Sharing an office

This can be an excellent option, providing a **stimulating working environment** at a **reasonable cost**. However, **your needs** and the needs of **your business** are **unique,** so consider the points in the following checklist to make sure it's right for you.

- ☐ Potential benefits vs. additional costs
- ☐ Dedicated workspace providing focus vs. lack of opportunity to personalize
- ☐ Commute – good or bad?
- ☐ Additional charge for resources, e.g. printers, internet connection, telephone/fax facilities?
- ☐ Shared office – motivating or distracting?
- ☐ Networking possibilities?
- ☐ Own desk or hot desk?
- ☐ Space for meetings?
- ☐ **Length** of the rental agreement? Early opt-out penalty?

If you think **sharing** an office might be the answer, use the checklist to help you **focus** on the **pros** and **cons** for your **specific** business.

If you decide this is the right approach for you, there are plenty of companies who can help you find a suitable venue, but treat it much as you would treat purchasing a new house.

* Take your time.
* Don't believe all the sales pitches.
* Visit several places before making your decision.

'**Environment is the mental feeding ground out of which the food that goes into our minds is extracted.**'
Napoleon Hill

Renting an office

If having a **dedicated** place of work is important to you but the idea of sharing an office **leaves you cold,** the answer might be to **rent** your own office.

* It is **more costly**, so you'll need to be clear about the perceived **benefits**.
* **Balance the cost** with the additional **value** the space gives you and your business.
* **Review** the situation regularly to see if it is matching up to your **expectations**.
* Ensure that the **terms of the lease** fit with your plans – short, medium and long term.
* Take your time to ensure that the office space is **exactly right** for your needs.

Review the situation regularly

Think carefully about the following questions.

1 What is your budget?
2 Would you prefer serviced or unserviced offices?
3 How important are your surroundings?
4 How large does your office need to be?
5 Does it cater for the needs of disabled employees, visitors, etc.?
6 Do you prefer privacy or a busy office environment?
7 How good are the communal facilities, e.g. toilets, meeting rooms, kitchen, etc.?
8 How good is the IT infrastructure?
9 For how long do you envisage renting the office space?

Creating the **right environment** is key to the **success** of your new business, providing:

* an inspiring environment
* a daily fillip to your working life
* a suitable corporate image.

Buying an office

This can be a good option if your business plans are long term, but obviously the costs (particularly up front) are significant.

Use this checklist to ensure that you have thought through the key points.

- ☐ You are signing up for a **long-term commitment**.
- ☐ If you need a mortgage, most lenders will require a **substantial deposit**.
- ☐ The **interest rate** on your mortgage can vary, making it **difficult to budget accurately**.
- ☐ Your premises will be subject to **fluctuations** in the property market.
- ☐ If your property increases in value, you may be liable to **capital gains tax**.
- ☐ You will be responsible for the **upkeep** of your office, inside and out.

34

Ask yourself – 'Am I **100 per cent certain** about buying an office?' If not, it's probably better to rent on a short-term contract to **see how it works out**. A rental agreement **opt-out clause** will allow you to purchase premises earlier if you decide that's the best way forward.

Remember
If you realize buying was a mistake, you will be lumbered with all the hassles, and costs, of selling your office – so only buy if you're certain it's the right move.

4 Targets and planning

Setting targets

It's crucial to establish a clear vision for your company from the outset, and to create a realistic **business plan** and **roadmap** to ensure that you get there. Adding **checkpoints** along the way will keep you on track and on target, and enable you to identify potential problems early.

When the going gets tough, and sometimes it will, you'll be able to remind yourself of your busines goals, and motivate yourself with tangible rewards for meeting targets.

It's crucial to establish a clear vision for your company

....

While determination and enthusiasm are vital when going solo, good **planning** is also a must. Without planning and setting targets you may struggle to succeed.

This chapter gives advice on:

* establishing a **vision** for your company
* understanding your company's **needs**
* identifying **potential problems** early – and how to solve them
* creating a **realistic business plan** and **roadmap**, with checkpoints
* setting realistic **targets** that don't aim too high or too low
* charting your position and **plotting a course** to meeting your targets
* **rewarding** yourself
* **broadcasting** your plans for added motivation.

Establishing a vision for your company

'Vision without action is a daydream. Action without vision is a nightmare.'

Japanese proverb

Crucial to the success of your business is your understanding of what you **want** from your company. You also need to know what you want your company and your offer to **look** like, and how you intend to **generate income** from it.

* Picture your company as you would like it to be:
    » at launch
    » in a year's time
    » in five years' time.

* Think through how it will operate:
    » day to day
    » month by month
    » year by year.

What do you need to **do** in order to **realize your vision?**

40

Problem solving

Large companies have the luxury of being able to afford to **make mistakes**, but you don't. You'll need to envisage **potential problems** and outline **strategies** for dealing with them. These will vary from business to business, so think through your plans carefully and decide what you would do if they occurred. For example:

What if...?	Coping strategy
Late payment	Do you have funds to cope?
Illness	Do you have backup? Insurance?
Cost increase	Can you pass this on to clients?

Business plan and roadmap

Structured planning will help you keep your business on track and provide an excellent yardstick by which to measure its progress.

A solid foundation for your business = a platform for success.

You will need to consider the following steps:

1 establishing your business offer
2 consolidating your initial start-up plans
3 creating a broad client base
4 managing cash flow
5 understanding your ultimate goal
6 deciding on a time frame for accomplishing it
7 measuring your progress.

Your roadmap should be organic, evolving over time, so you'll need to re-evaluate your business plan regularly and be crystal clear as to what you want to achieve, and by when.

Optimism versus realism

> **'The pessimist complains about the wind; the optimist expects it to change; the realist adjusts the sails.'**
>
> William Arthur Ward

Ensure that your **targets** are as **realistic** as possible, given your:

* starting capital
* experience
* ability
* available time
* resources
* timing (prevailing market conditions)
* contacts and initial clients.

Be **honest** and **tough** with yourself – it will save you much completely **avoidable disappointment** later. Aiming unrealistically high is a great way to make you feel like a **failure**, even if you are doing **well**. Equally, don't aim low simply to ensure that you reach your targets!

Charting your position and plotting a course

Mark your targets and deadlines on a **wall planner** to remind yourself where your company is, where it needs to be, and by when. This makes it easy to assess your under- or over-achievement versus plan. First, determine your growth potential.

Broadcast your forecast
No one likes to fall short of their targets – and everyone loathes doing so publicly.

	Current position	Ultimate future
Where is your company?		
What does it look like?		
How many people does it employ?		
What does your client roster comprise?		
What is your business worth?		

Next, **plot the points** between these two positions.

* How will you **grow** the company?
* What are the necessary **steps** along the way?
* What **stepping stones** are required?

* Where will they be?
* What **help** will you need?
* What are the potential **obstacles**?
* What's the **timescale**?

Now you have everything you need to plot your company's course to its **maximum growth potential** and every reason to believe you can get it there.

✔ *You know **where** your business is.*
✔ *You know where you **want** it to be.*
✔ *You know the **requisite steps** along the way.*

✔ *You know what **assistance** you'll need.*
✔ *You know **how** you'll **achieve** your goals.*
✔ *You know the **timescale** for each.*

Motivation

> 'People unable to motivate themselves must be content with mediocrity, no matter how impressive their other talents.'
>
> Andrew Carnegie

The stick

List all the reasons you wanted to jettison working for someone else, such as:

* **commuting**
* office **politics**
* being **told** what to do
* working hard to line **someone else's** pockets
* wanting to **call the shots**
* wanting your **own style** for the business
* wanting **flexibility**
* wanting a better **work–life balance**.

Bullet Guide: Work for Yourself

The carrot

Plan in some **realistic** and **tangible rewards** for yourself, to **celebrate** each successful milestone.

	Quarter	Year end	Long term
Completion date	30 June	31 December	Within next 10 years
Project/sales target	Jazz / £8,000	Minimum of 6 / £32,000	8 global / £250,000 per year
Reward	Day at the races	Weekend at luxury hotel	Ferrari

CASE STUDY: Taking time off

'At the end of every quarter I take time off to reward myself. This is not a weekend thing – it only takes time from my work diary. It is worth every minute as it energizes me for the next quarter.' (UK)

Top tip

When the going gets tough, remember *why* you started your own business.

5 Working 5-9

What is 5–9 working?

This way of working (working from 5 p.m. to 9 p.m.) means **combining paid employment** with running your own company in your **spare time**, and can offer the best of both worlds.

The latest technology is making this an increasingly viable – and attractive – option for many people. It also affords you the opportunity to **test** your business in the **marketplace** before making it your only source of income.

Working 5–9 can offer the best of both worlds
....

This chapter looks at the **benefits and drawbacks** of working 5–9. It describes:

* the **enterprise renaissance**, and the reasons for this growing **trend**
* the importance of clear objectives – will you have a lucrative **hobby** or the foundation of a successful **business**?
* the additional **challenge** of 5–9 working
* making 5–9 working **work for you**
* **testing the market** through 5–9 working.

Benefits and drawbacks of 5-9 working

You'll need to be aware of the drawbacks as well as the benefits of combining a full- or part-time job with running your business in your spare time.

Benefits

✔ Become your own boss **gradually**
✔ Establish your business at your **own pace**
✔ You don't need to rely on its profits for your livelihood
✔ You have freedom to **experiment** with your offer

Drawbacks

✘ Number of **hours** which need to be worked
✘ **Decrease** in spare time
✘ Loss of **social life**
✘ Not devoting **100%** of your time to your business

'There's nothing like biting off more than you can chew, and then chewing anyway.'
Mark Burnett

52

The enterprise renaissance

An increasing number of entrepreneurs are running a **business** in their **spare time** while remaining in full-time or part-time employment. Reasons include:

* fears about the economy
* possibility of redundancy
* difficulties of securing start-up bank loans
* potential offered by the latest technology
* desire to be in control
* desire for financial security.

More than **5 million** people in the UK are currently earning some form of income **from home,** and the number is **steadily increasing**. In the US the figure for this kind of self-employment is more than 10 million. Social media as well as technological advances mean it's never been easier to start a part-time business on a very small budget.

Lucrative hobby or successful career?

Firstly, you will need to be **clear** about your **objectives** for your 5–9 business. There are two **common routes**:

* ✳ keeping it as a **hobby**
    * » the thrill of running your own business is reward enough
    * » you don't want the pressure of needing your business to support you financially
* ✳ making it your **career**
    * » you want to be able to give up your day job
    * » you are convinced that there is scope for your business to become your career.

If you fall into the **second category** (and most people do), you'll need to have an **accurate projection** of when you expect your business to be **able to support** you.

Be clear about your objectives for your 5–9 business

The additional challenge of 5–9 working

All the same rules apply as they would if you were taking the leap to working for yourself full time straight away, but you will face one additional challenge: the **long hours** will eat into your leisure time.

> *If I'm spending all my spare time working, how will I maintain a social life – and find enough time to sleep?*

'Hard work spotlights the character of people: some turn up their sleeves, some turn up their noses, and some don't turn up at all.'
Sam Ewing

Top tip
Don't underestimate how much work you'll need to do to get your business off the ground. Many 5–9 workers put in at least as many hours on their 'part-time' business as on their full-time job.

Making 5–9 working work for you

If you are prepared to put in the long hours and the hard work, then working 5–9 can be a great way to get started as your own boss. However…

Caution!

Plenty of **guides** to part-time working suggest possible **business opportunities** you might like to consider, such as:

* private tutoring
* life coaching
* catering
* virtual PA.

However, if you are **unsure** about:

* the type of company you should start
* what your offer should be
* the nature of the work you should do,

you may not be **sufficiently prepared** to launch your own company, or **sufficiently passionate** about your new business to make it **successful**.

56

The hard reality of 5-9 working

Imagine a **long day** at work followed by **hours more working** at home; and at weekends working **9–5** on your business and possibly **5–9** as well.

> **'When I was young, I observed that nine out of ten things I did were failures. So I did ten times more work.'**
>
> George Bernard Shaw

Top tip
If you are not truly passionate about your new business, putting in the hours and covering the hard yards will seem very hard indeed.

Testing the market

Starting your business by working 5–9 can be particularly valuable if you are **unsure** of the **commercial viability** of your idea and wish to **test it** on the market before **quitting** your job.

> ### Top tip
> Use this time to rigorously assess whether your idea needs to remain a pipe dream, or whether it can become a profitable business.

Your **business idea** may be a long-held **dream** in which you may well have already **invested** a good deal of:

* time
* hope
* ambition

* emotion
* energy
* money.

However, you must be **brutally honest** with yourself about its **chances of success**.

Your idea is not commercially viable

Be honest with yourself; **painful** as it is to have your business **dreams shattered**, it's far more painful to **ignore the warning signs** and carry on regardless

Continue with your 5–9 business as an **enjoyable hobby**

Reassess your business proposition and **try again**

Your idea is commercially viable

Assess the **risk** involved in **giving up your job** to run the business **full time**

Continue to **test** and **refine** your offer

Quit your job and **commit** yourself fully to your **new enterprise**

'Most of us can easily do two things at once; what's all but impossible is to do one thing at once.'

Mignon McLaughlin

6 Maximizing the advantages of working for yourself

Accentuating the positives

There are both significant **upsides** and significant **downsides** to working for yourself, so you will need to learn how to **maximize the advantages** while **minimizing the disadvantages**. The trick is to turn every difference between your situation and that of big businesses to your advantage.

You can also create a work structure that really works for you – and you get to **make all the rules**!

There are both upsides and downsides to working for yourself

This chapter looks at:

* the **advantages** of small (and how to negate the **disadvantages**)
* your **strengths** versus larger businesses
* the advantages of **making the rules**
* shaping your work life
* the disadvantages of making the rules
* **downtime**, and how to use it to your advantage
* the importance of taking holidays.

The advantages of small

It is important to **analyse** your business's situation and identify its **strengths and weaknesses** versus the competition – particularly that from **larger** businesses. How does your **company's size** give you advantages, and how can you best **exploit** them?

* Focus on your **strengths** as a **small** enterprise.
* Analyse any **large** competitor's **weaknesses** as a big enterprise.
* Determine how to **turn** the situation to **your advantage**.
* **Avoid** going toe to toe with them in **a straight fight**.
* Capitalize on your **speed** and **mobility** to:
    » win projects **ahead** of them
    » take on the projects that they deem **too small** and fiddly.

Focus on your strengths

The exact advantages and disadvantages will vary from business to business, but the **principles** remain constant.

* You are **smaller** so you can't outgun them – but being smaller makes you more **flexible**.
* You are less established and **less well known** – which means you are **fresher** and can offer something genuinely **new** and **different**.
* You are on your own – so you are not **slowed** down by an **inefficient** chain of command.
* You probably don't have **swanky** offices, which makes you more **cost-effective**.

The advantages of making your own rules

Since you're the boss and can make the rules, enjoy the **flexibility** of your new working life and **tailor** it exactly the way **you want**. Just be careful that you're completing as much work as you need to and that it's of the required quality.

You can:

* work your own **hours/days/weeks**, as it suits you
* **pick** and **choose** the work you want to do
* **dress** and, indeed, **behave** the way you want to
* take as many **breaks** as you want, whenever you want, and go wherever you want to enjoy them
* make all the business decisions; no one else is telling you what to do or how to do it
* make the most of the opportunity to **pursue** more **creative** and **imaginative** work interests.

You should also try to ensure that you:

* achieve an optimum **work–life balance**
* **schedule** your working life to benefit from an increase in **quality time** when and where it counts
* enjoy the **challenge** of being your own boss and the opportunity for **self-growth**
* use your work–life **freedom** to help **shape** your life **positively**.

CASE STUDY: Freedom to choose

'I think my most uncomfortable moment was a piece of work for a huge company that was a former nationalized industry/utility. They were a nightmare – incredibly bureaucratic, inconsiderate and demanding. But the great thing is that I don't have to work for them again if I choose not to.'(Sole trader, UK)

The disadvantages of making the rules

Taking a close look at the **disadvantages** of working for yourself can help to ensure you're prepared to tackle them and even highlight ways of **turning them into an advantage**.

Reality of working for yourself	Disadvantage	Opportunity
Working **alone**	Loneliness	Attend **workshops/courses** **Network**
Blank work canvas	No clear work life **structure**	Paint the **future** as **you** want it **Clarify** your **vision** and **roadmap** **Create** a structure that **really works** for you
Loss of **IT** infrastructure/support	Have to start **from scratch**	Install a set-up which precisely **matches** your **requirements**
Financial insecurity	**Fear** of insolvency	**Structure** your **business** effectively **Keep** all the **rewards** of your efforts

Another **disadvantage** is that when you're working for yourself you need to be **completely self-reliant**…

CASE STUDY: Getting help

'I call it the cup of tea syndrome. There is no one to make you a cup of tea and that applies to everything. So you have to get focused on a) what you are good at and b) what you aren't, and ensure you get help with the latter…'(Sole trader, New Zealand)

Downtime, and how to use it to your advantage

When you work for yourself **you are your business**.

What is it that occupies your thoughts even when you should be enjoying a well-earned break?

70

> **Top tip**
> Avoid the temptation to be 'at work' all the time – it is no good for you or your business. *Everyone* needs some downtime.

1 trying to **crack a problem** on the latest project?
2 trying to think of **new routes** to getting work?
3 trying to decide how best to **handle a client**?
4 wondering whether – or how – to chase an **outstanding invoice**?

You need to have an **'off' switch** – and discipline yourself to **use it**.

Taking holidays

You will naturally feel **apprehensive**, especially at first, about **leaving your business** for any length of time. Nevertheless, if you want it – and yourself – to thrive in the long term, you must **learn to let go**.

Top tip
Your business won't grind to a halt if you're not there to babysit it every second of every day.

At the very least you should take a **long weekend** here and there. Go away when work is slow anyway, and grab a last-minute bargain!

> **'The best part of a holiday is perhaps not so much to be resting yourself, as to see all the other fellows busy working.'**
> Kenneth Grahame

7 Finance

Managing your finances

One of the most important tasks you face when you work for yourself is successfully structuring and managing your business's finances. It's therefore worth spending the time and effort to get it right.

Remember that **every business is different**, so you'll need to determine your company's financial needs and your aspirations for its future growth. **Aim high**, certainly, but remember to be **realistic** as well.

Determine your company's financial needs and your aspirations for its future growth
....

This chapter gives you practical advice on managing your **finances**, including:

* what to consider when you start
* information about different **trading methods**
* keeping your company's **books**
* how to decide whether you need an **accountant**
* financial housekeeping
* getting the right type – and level – of **insurance**.

Getting started

It's never too early to start getting your new business's **finances** in order when you work for yourself. Begin by making a list of your **business requirements**, which should include the following steps.

1 Arrange sufficient **initial capital**.
2 Set up your **company bank account**.
3 Estimate your likely **running costs**.
4 Establish a sound **financial framework** for your business.
5 Plan your **business growth** with realistic **profit forecasts**.

'If you have to forecast, forecast often.'
Edgar R. Fiedler

To ensure that your cash flow never **haemorrhages,** you'll need to have arranged:

* ongoing **working capital**
* a **contingency** fund.

You should only ever dip into your **personal savings** to help your business in a **real emergency** – and then **only with great caution**. If you do, it's important to remember two things:

1 your forecast was **inaccurate** (determine why, to prevent the situation recurring)
2 you have only **loaned** your company the money.

If you need to secure a short-term **bank loan,** first be sure that you have a sufficiently robust **repayment vehicle** in place.

> Until your business is able to repay you, it's insolvent.

Which trading method?

There are two **common trading methods,** and you'll need to decide which one is best suited to **your needs,** taking into account such factors as:

* level of **risk**
* degree of **capital investment** required
* **financial** implications
* **benefits and drawbacks** over the short, medium and long term.

	Biggest benefit	Biggest drawback
Sole trader (the technical term for being self-employed)	Simplicity	You're personally liable for all your business debts
Limited company	Protection	Additional bureaucracy and cost

Many accountants will model each trading method according to your business's projection to help determine the best one for you.

Your company's books

Keeping your company's accounts is a necessary evil, but regularly keeping on top of them will be much **less hassle** in the long run.

Accurate accounts are vital to your company's success. They will:

* ensure you pay the **correct amount** of tax
* provide a **yardstick** to your **profitability**.

Keeping your accounts:

* **accurate**
* **up to date**
* **easy to read**

> **Top tip**
> You don't have to be an expert, but make sure you understand the basics of accountancy and business finance.

provides an important **measure of** your company's historic, current and future **success** or lack of it. It is also a **legal requirement** in most countries.

Do you need an accountant?

When you first begin working for yourself, you will:

* be very **busy**
* have numerous **demands** on your **time**.

You may not know:

* exactly what records you need to keep
* how they should be set out
* how to complete tax return forms
* how much time to allow.

There is little doubt that an **experienced accountant** can **save you time** and **effort,** but you'll need to balance this against the **additional cost** to your business.

Top tip
Employing an accountant, even for just a year, will provide you with a pro forma for your accounts that you can use in subsequent years.

Is **hiring an accountant** worth the **cost**? First, you'll need to determine the importance of the **benefits**.

You will:

* have your accounts completed in the correct way, on time, and looking professional
* very probably save money.

Top tip
Ask other owners of small businesses to recommend a reputable accountant.

You won't have to:

* complete the taxation forms yourself
* do the complex calculations.

CASE STUDY: The cost of not hiring an accountant

'When I first began I decided not to use an accountant. After six months of struggling I was losing more money by spending so much time on the bookkeeping than it would have cost me to have employed someone!' (Sole trader, Germany)

Financial housekeeping

Keep your bookkeeping as **straightforward** as possible.

* **Set aside sufficient funds to pay your tax bills.**
  Your taxes are no longer collected as you earn, and you'll need to pay a lump sum annually.
* **Ensure your business's funds are easily accessible.**
  Keep some of your company's money in an instant-access account to ensure an uninterrupted cash flow.
* **Keep all your receipts.**
  Offset against your taxes **expenses** incurred **solely** and **wholly** for the purposes of your **business**.
* **Keep your company's books up to date.**
  Make life easy for yourself by always having an **accurate measurement** of **how well** your company is performing versus **forecast**.

Insurance

> **'An economist is an expert who will know tomorrow why the things he predicted yesterday didn't happen today.'**
>
> Laurence J. Peter

In case of **emergencies**, it's **important** to have **adequate insurance** in place to cover you and your business. The **range** of products on offer can be **mind-boggling** (as can prices), so take time to find the **right one**. Ask yourself the following questions:

Does my business require me to have a lot of expensive stock?

Do I need indemnity insurance?

Do I need personal insurance cover?

Having appropriate insurance cover will give you peace of mind.

8 Effective home working

Maximizing home-office potential

Working from home can save **time** and **money**, as well as offering **home comforts**. However, using your home as your office leaves you prone to constant interruptions and home life **temptations**. Finding the right **balance** between home life and work life – for you, for anyone who lives with you, and for your business – is crucial to your success.

Working from home leaves you prone to constant interruptions

. . . .

This chapter looks at the issues arising from using your **home** as your **office**. It lists the advantages and disadvantages, and offers advice on how to:

* achieve the best **work–life balance**
* ring-fence **time** and **space**
* create the right **environment for work**
* maximize **efficiency** in your workspace
* **take exercise**, even while at your desk
* avoid **prevarication and transference**.

Using your home as your office

Using your **home** as your **office** offers both **advantages** and **drawbacks**:

Advantages
* Closer to **family** and **friends**
* No commuting
* Able to create an **ideal** working environment
* Work life **flexibility**

Drawbacks
* Temptation to become **sidetracked** by home life
* Home life **interruptions**
* Loss of **focus**
* Loss of work life **framework**

88

CASE STUDY: How to be disciplined

'Firstly, you need to be efficient – not mixing business and domestic material, etc. Secondly, you need to have a room that does not feel too homely; otherwise you'll be prone to slips of discipline. Never, ever work within earshot of a television!' (Sole trader, UK)

Achieving work–life balance

Since home life and work life **occupy the same space** for home-alone workers, it's important to develop strategies to **separate them**. Initially this can be **problematic,** especially as the technologies for working are always available, and you'll usually find that one is **eclipsing** the other. When this happens, follow these steps.

1 Ascertain the **optimum** work–life balance for you, your family, and your business's needs.
2 Determine which area is taking **too much** of the share, and to **what degree**.
3 **Identify patterns** that are causing problems and establish the reasons.
4 With all appropriate parties, create an **action plan** to remedy the imbalance.
5 Put the plan into **action** and **monitor** the situation.
6 **Adjust** as necessary.

Time and space

> Company is important.
> But so is your company.

Time

Ensure that you **ring-fence** your time so that your working day isn't eroded by visitors. Agree simple **rules** about when it's okay to disturb you – and implement firm **boundaries** for yourself. To protect your time, try adopting a 'closed office door' policy.

Ensure that you ring-fence your time

CASE STUDY: Setting boundaries

'We made some rules about when it was okay for my family to disturb me, and vice versa. It seems odd making boundaries in your own home, with your own family, but it would be impossible for me to work from home if we didn't have them.' (Home worker, Germany)

Space

Establishing a clear **demarcation** between your **office** (work) space and your **home** (life) space is crucial to putting yourself mentally into **'work mode'**. It also creates a clear **boundary** that other members of your household will acknowledge. You'll have more control over your own separate space, and you'll also be able more easily to leave your work life behind whenever you leave your workspace.

CASE STUDY: A dedicated space

'Having a separate office really helps – I shut my door and I'm in my own working world. It is *my* working environment – to inspire and stimulate. I can go there at 4 a.m. and nobody notices…'
(Home worker, USA)

Creating the right environment

Your office should look and feel like a workspace, propelling you into work mode the moment you cross the threshold.

* Turn permanent fixtures into practical **office furniture** (e.g. wardrobes into store cupboards).
* Decorate in **neutral** tones.
* Choose a **plain outlook**, to minimize distractions.
* **Avoid** furniture that doubles for **domestic** duties (e.g. a sofa bed which turns your office into a guest bedroom).
* Install sufficient **storage** such as shelving and filing cabinets.
* Ensure it's **well lit**.
* Fix **blinds** instead of curtains.
* Keep **ornaments** and **knick-knacks** to a minimum.

'Be careful of the environment you choose, for it will shape you.'

W. Clement Stone

Maximizing efficiency in your workspace

If you don't have a spare room for your office and your workspace has to cohabit with your living space, you'll need to ensure that it looks and feels **different** and that you don't allow your work life and home life to merge.

CASE STUDY: Improving productivity

'When I started working from home I watched television while I worked. It was great – until I realized my productivity had halved. Now I work at my desk every day and my productivity is back up to 100 per cent.' (Home worker, France)

Top tip

If your workspace blends with your home space, one will simply disappear, and it will almost always be the workspace.

Exercise at work

People who take regular exercise tend to be more productive and less stressed than those who don't. Keeping **active** is important for:

> An active body = an active mind

* positive mental stimulus
* keeping your brain healthy
* keeping your outlook and your ideas fresh.

Taking time off for daily **exercise** will:

* 'blow away the cobwebs'
* give you **perspective** (on current work, and your business as a whole)
* release **tension** and endorphins
* change your **scenery**
* give you a mental **break**
* **recharge** your batteries
* keep you **healthy**.

Top tip
The Royal Canadian Air Force's 'Exercise Plans For Physical Fitness' only need 15 minutes each day – and you don't even need to leave your desk.

94

Avoiding prevarication and transference

'**To do**' lists aid organization and workload prioritization, provided they're kept **short**, relevant and realistic. Making **long** lists of things you plan to do is a fantastic way of ensuring that you never do them.

Long lists = transference.
Transference = getting nowhere fast.

Study list of ten things to achieve

Realize you're back where you started

Enjoy feeling of accomplishment

Ditch old list

Transfer six remaining items from old list

The 'transference trap'

Lump three together – rewrite list

Postpone two things until tomorrow

Add four new items to a new list

9 IT for the solo worker

The connected world

We are truly in the age of **instant access**, **instant response connectivity**, 24/7, with zero downtime. Used appropriately, it can provide a **lifeline** to you and your business. Moreover, it is something your clients are likely to expect and something that can boost your **productivity** and **efficiency**, and help to project an image of **accessibility** and **professionalism**.

We are truly in the age of instant access, instant response connectivity

While it may be easy to stay in touch with your suppliers and clients, it's important to implement only the **IT solutions** that are going to be the **most useful** to you, so that you don't waste money. This chapter looks at:

* information gathering
* communication
* connectivity
* data management
* mobile working
  » increased flexibility
  » minimizing costs
  » 'virtual' businesses
  » streamlining your working practices.

Information gathering

Thanks to the **internet**, it has never been easier to **research** and gather information via **powerful** and increasingly **accurate search engines**, while **Wikipedia**, the world's surely most comprehensive encyclopaedia, is never more than a few clicks away.

Caution!

The World Wide Web can be dangerously addictive. 'Surfing' (skipping contentedly from website to website) can cost countless working hours if you're not wise to the risk and careful to implement your own internet rules of engagement.

> **'Anyone who has lost track of time when using a computer knows the propensity to dream, the urge to make dreams come true and the tendency to miss lunch.'**
>
> Tim Berners-Lee

Communication

We are in the age of continuous and never-ending contact and, whether we like it or not, it's something that's increasingly expected and demanded by clients, customers, suppliers and even colleagues. Some of the most popular communication tools are:

* mobile 'phone
* telephone landline
* email
* Skype.

Record your own **voicemail** message to:

* **customize** your greeting
* reflect the **personality** of your company
* make a good **first impression**
* ensure that customers know they got the **right number** and that you got their **message**.

> **Top tip**
> Setting up **dedicated** numbers and addresses will make your business look **professional** and allow you to **prioritize** your communications.

Connectivity

It's crucial to stay in touch with your business, suppliers and clients in order to keep track of demands and facilitate active communication. Here are some of the more common connectivity business tools:

Connectivity tool	Priority	Advantages	Disadvantages
Website	High	* High **profile** * Clearly **illustrate** your offer	* Time-consuming set-up * Potentially **complicated**
Blog	Medium	* Virtual business **soapbox**	* Must be updated regularly
Facebook	Medium	* Two-way communication * **Leverage** social networking	* Must incorporate social element
Twitter	Low	* **Constant** client connection	* High maintenance
YouTube	Low	* **Video** connectivity	* Finding enough material
Viral **games**, **apps**, etc.	Low	* Entertaining	* Expensive * Long lead times

102

Data management

There are multiple ways to **back up** and **store data**, such as:

* server
* external hard drive
* USB data stick (dongle)
* DVD.

Warning!

It's crucial that you back up your data regularly so that you never find yourself in the business-stalling situation of a mid-project data loss.

A complete copy of the latest state of your hard drive really is one of those things you never fully appreciate until you need it.

Mobile working

Increased flexibility

Working for yourself gives you the flexibility to work virtually anywhere you please, whenever you wish, and in any number of ways. Your office is truly mobile when you are armed with a selection of:

* mobile phone
* Blackberry
* iPhone
* wireless connectivity **laptop**
* **3G** dongle.

You can even work on the move permanently, if you decide that this peripatetic style of working makes the best use of your time and resources.

This ability to **shake up your routine** not only makes working more pleasant, but it can also help **boost your business productivity**. To your clients you're always 'at the office', allowing them **instant access** to you and your business.

104

Minimizing costs

Although getting set up with a fully flexible working arrangement will involve some **upfront costs**, it's an **investment** that can soon **pay for itself**.

Ask yourself the following questions:

Which communication/connectivity tools do I really need?

Which tools does my business require from the outset?

Do I really need the best available, or will a cheaper alternative do?

Top tip
Winning work you might otherwise have lost out on is the ultimate cost-saving measure.

The other side to minimizing costs is revenue generation; an efficient mobile working set-up can help you gain new work and new clients.

'Virtual' businesses

As your own boss in sole charge of your business, you can project whatever image of **your company's profile** you choose.

Mobile working enables you to **create** and **maintain** an *image* of your company that perfectly reflects the **ideal situation** – and if your work is good what should it matter what your office space looks like?

Top tip

Picture your business as you'd like it to be. Try to see it from all angles so that you build up a three-dimensional model, one that you really see and believe in. Commit it to memory, so that whenever you talk about your business this is **the image you convey**.

Picture your business as you'd like it to be

Streamlining your working practices

Capitalize on the flexibility of mobile working, by ensuring that you always **have to hand** all the work you need to complete so that you can work on **logical groups** of workpieces, wherever you are.

> Eliminating the need to cherry-pick your work sequence means streamlining your working practices, which will make you more efficient and more effective.

1 Identify which tasks can be **combined**.
2 Determine how **often** they need to be completed.
3 **Prioritize** them.
4 **Action** them.

Top tip
Avoid wasting time through physical and mental transition from one task to another. With small tasks, a transition period can equal or even exceed the time required to complete the tasks themselves.

10 Dealing with clients

The supplier–client relationship

Securing and **retaining clients** is fundamental to every business in one way or another. Learning the necessary skills is vital to business success, especially if you are working for yourself.

Understanding your **clients' needs** and how you can help them, building **lasting relationships**, adding genuine **value** to their business and ensuring that you become **indispensable** to them are all necessary elements to the **long-term success** of your business.

Securing and retaining clients is fundamental to every business
....

This chapter gives you advice on:

* **recruiting** clients for the short, medium and long term
* retaining clients
* fostering one-to-one **relationships**
* what to do when you are being **ignored** by your clients
* **balancing** your workload
* **aligning** your offer and becoming **indispensable**
* how to get **paid early**
* **fighting** your corner – and **winning**.

Recruitment of clients

*Q: What are your **three priorities** when starting to work for yourself?*

*A: 1. Your **first** client. 2. Your **second** client. 3. Your **third** client.*

You'll need to win clients for your new business as quickly as possible, to **generate revenue** and establish your **reputation**.

1 Attract clients **before you begin** your business, preferably those who know your work.
2 Obtain **word-of-mouth** recommendations from existing clients.
3 Make **cold** approaches.

Since you can never have too many clients, it's best to do all three.

Personal recommendations are far better than cold advertising – easier to implement, cheaper, and more likely to be successful.

Retention of clients

Establishing a client base is your most difficult task. Just as important, however, is the retention of clients, vital to business success over the long term. To facilitate this, you'll need to:

* provide outstanding **service**
* **price** yourself competitively
* maintain regular **contact**
* predict your clients' needs – and provide **solutions**
* build **lasting relationships**.

If clients get what they **need**, **enjoy** working with you and **trust** you they'll use you again and again.

You can never have too many clients

Fostering one-to-one relationships

An excellent **business relationship** is more than just the relationship between companies; it's the **personal relationship** you establish with one or two specific people at each company. Get to know your clients as **individuals**:

* what makes them tick
* what they need
* what they most appreciate/ dislike in a supplier.

> How often have you heard the phrase 'It's a people business'? The truth is *every* business is a people business.

This will:

* give you the inside track to gaining further work
* allow you to give them outstanding customer service
* cement your client/supplier relationship
* allow you to predict, and circumvent, possible roadblocks to gaining future work.

Being ignored

Sometimes your calls won't be returned. When this happens…

Do

✔ *persevere*
✔ *try to find out why*
✔ *appear supportive*

Don't

✘ *become frustrated*
✘ *become a nuisance*
✘ *give up*

There is no sentiment in business, and a little healthy scepticism can:

✽ keep your expectations **realistic**
✽ ensure that you always have **sufficient work** lined up.

Top tip
If you expect clients to honour every firm commitment, you are likely to be very disappointed very often.

'A verbal contract isn't worth the paper it's written on.'
Samuel Goldwyn

Balancing your workload

Two of the biggest challenges you'll face are:

* too much work
* not enough work.

Both can be **detrimental** to

> Getting the balance right is notoriously difficult due to the **feast or famine** nature of working for yourself.

your business, or even conspire to cripple it. There are likely to be few occasions when you get the balance just right; the key is not to let the pendulum swing too far in either direction.

CASE STUDY: Workload

'Having too little work is a terrible thing for a soloist. It undermines your confidence, your prospects and your bank balance. But just as bad is having too much on.' (Home worker, UK)

Aligning your offer and becoming indispensable

It's vital that you fully understand your **client's needs** rather than simply trying to foist your core offer on them because 'it's what you do'. To produce consistently excellent, targeted work, you'll need to:

1 get a thorough **brief**
2 decide whether to **modify** your offer to make it **relevant**
3 ensure that you're not sacrificing the **integrity** of your core offer.

However, in order to become **indispensable** you'll need to:

1 **pre-empt** your clients' needs
2 identify **challenges** their businesses will face
3 provide the **answers**.

This way you become more than simply a service provider: you become an indispensable part of their business.

Getting paid early

Late payments represent a major obstacle to the smooth running of any business. So how can you ensure prompt – or even early – payment?

1 Ensure that all costs, including expenses, are **agreed in full *and in writing*** before you begin any work.
2 Ensure that you have agreed the **timescale** for payment.
3 Insist on receiving a **purchase order** number.
4 **Submit** your invoice at the earliest opportunity.
5 Once submitted, check to make sure your invoice **arrived safely.**
6 **Chase** your payment *before* it is due.
7 Foster a **one-to-one relationship** with someone in the **accounts** department.
8 **Thank** your clients for prompt payment.

Fighting your corner

Beware clients **haggling** over costs! Don't lower your day/hourly rate. Instead, look at ways to pare down your process so it takes **less time**. In this way:

* the **cost/time** ratio is unaltered
* you haven't reduced your perceived **worth**
* you've met your client's **budget** requirements
* you've set a **remuneration precedent** for the future.

CASE STUDY: The perils of undercharging

'In my first year I wasn't confident enough to charge the right day rate. Subsequently I have never been able to get back to those clients with my correct day rate and, even more importantly, they do not value my work as highly as my other clients. A bad mistake.' (Entrepreneur, UK)